DEDICATION
To Willard Morss   1898-1989

Thanks, Grandpa Willard for listening to, recording
and believing the Indian's waterfall legend told to
your father, Samuel Morss on the Hoh River in 1919.

With this third publication of "<u>STOLEN PRINCESS</u>",
The "chiefs", mothers, princes, and princesses of the
Morss, Herren, and Jacobson families have come to
love your stories and the memories they invoke as
your legacy, another set of footprints in the sand.

And though you and Grandma Camilla left us in 1988-89
we "Hope 2 C U B 4 2 long!"

--Janet Morss Herren/Waller

STOLEN PRINCESS
A Northwest Indian Legend

By
Willard Morss

&

Janet Morss Herren

ISBN: 0-6159-9933-6
ISBN-13: 9780615999333

Published by JM Herren
Janetherren@comcast.net

CONTENTS

Samuel Benjamin Morss   1860 — 1920
Frances Elliot Wallace   1865 — 1955

INTRODUCTION
The Olympic Peninsula

Water...sand...sky...the in-and-out ritual of sea and tide responding daily to the clock first wound by the Creator, the migration of the salmon...berries blooming and bearing...trees reaching high...snows falling and melting. These facets of the diamond of the Olympic Peninsula we have with us still.

But what of the people, the earliest man who made his home along the beaches and streams of the peninsula before the coming of the overland explorer, and the strange seaborne invader? We have only a folklore of legends handed down verbally from one generation to another, a few carved totems and scattered artifacts to make up their meager history. Some of the legends — rich in culture, tasting and smelling of nature — ring of the true exploit and adventure. Others border on the fantastic.

Or is it fantastic that an Indian maiden could cause a mountain waterfall to move from its original location, an undertaking that would be considered a major engineering feat today? The Princess accomplished this without even trying, according to the story told to a passing stranger by one of her descendants in the summer of 1919. That stranger was my father, Samuel B. Morss, a country preacher and carpenter.

Dad was living in the Grays Harbor country at the time he heard the legend. Those who knew of his love of photography urged him to take his summer vacation on the Olympic Peninsula, where the Olympic Mountains reigned over the coastal vista. He chose to make the "loop trip", going by way of Bremerton and Port Angeles to the very tip of Cape Flattery, before turning south and hiking down the coast and then home.

Good weather was with him. He carried a small pack of bare essentials with his camera. To avoid the cool night breezes from the Pacific he would build his campfires in the shelter of the driftwood. Mountain streams from Alaska to California had sent timbers out to sea, only to have wind and tide bring them ashore to form the weathered barricade along the high tideline. It was here Dad huddled one night toward the end of his journey...

He absentmindedly ground the sand crystals between his teeth as he read beside his fire. The wind gently lifted his hair, and flipped the silken pages of his worn Bible from mid-Jeremiah to somewhere in the New Testament. Thunderous waves left their vibrations along the shore and withdrew again with a soft "hiss, hiss."

The abrupt intrusion of the stranger's boots into the firelight did not frighten him — he had been welcome in the Indian towns during his beach hike. But as he looked up at the young Indian he was suddenly aware of the expensive camera in his pack. He sat up now as the stranger spoke:

"You are the man who fixed my father's saw this morning?" Relieved by the reference to the saw-sharpening incident, Dad stood and put out his hand. He guessed his age to be thirteen or so. There was a strong fish scent about him, probably from the boots. But the plaid wool mackinaw and heavy pants were clean, and very similar to his own clothes. His black hair was tied back neatly.

"That was your father?" Dad asked. The man nodded.

"I was merely sympathizing with a fellow carpenter, trying to use a rusty saw. I took it over to the salmon cannery where they loaned me a file."

"I know," replied the Indian, "my father is glad to have a sharp saw again." He started to turn away when Dad said:

"Wait — excuse my poor manners. Please, sit down and have a cup of tea with me. And let me introduce myself. I'm Sam Morss from Hoquiam." The Indian smiled now and accepted the cup Dad poured for him.

"I am Jimmy Goodman. You were kind to help my father."

"Well now I believe that's what we're here for — to help others whenever we can." (He tapped his Bible.) "I am a preacher by trade. Your father did me a great favor too, by ferrying me across the river in his canoe. I had been warned that these river mouths can be treacherous."

"Tides and undertow, and the current — you should be careful. It is better to go upstream and cross if you have to." Jimmy was looking at Dad's pack behind him on the log.

"My father says you took his picture."

"Yes, I've taken many pictures — that's the reason for my trip. I had heard about the mountains and coastline, and I have found the scenery beyond all expectations. To look at those rugged peaks one has to believe that some great Master Hand has carved them with a giant chisel. I would like to hike through them one day."

Jimmy's response was enthusiastic:

"You should see some of the lakes — water as blue as the lupine flower, streams and waterfalls that make such noise, you and I could not speak above it. I could take you there...two days." He paused to stir the fire, giving Dad time to think.

"Well now, Jimmy, that's a fine offer. But I'm afraid I must be home again by this Sunday. 'Been away from my church for three Sundays now." Jimmy nodded and set down his empty cup.

"And I must go back to school soon, too." He mentioned his school at La Push. Dad was intrigued, and urged him to stay and talk about his Quileute background. Jimmy reached for a piece of firewood, and sat down again. He began to talk about his brothers, and how his family still relied on salmon fishing for their living.

"So much has changed since the Government came and built the school. It seems the teachers want us to learn the white man's words and forget our own. There is so little left of our culture — the fire of '88 destroyed all written word of our people, and masks, tools, baskets — everything. Now my brothers and cousins all try to remember the stories of our fathers we have heard at the potlatches. It is all we have left." Dad read the sadness and the reverence for the past in Jimmy's words. He was impressed with the wisdom of the young man's short years.

And thus on a warm summer night in 1919, on the beach near the mouth of the Hoh River, my father listened as Jimmy Goodman told of his ancestors, and then close the evening with the legend you are about to read, of *"The Little Princess and the Waterfall."* It was a perfect setting for the story — sound of surf and gulls enveloping teller and listener as they shared the fading warmth of the fire.

"The story is true," said Jimmy with a slight smile; "the water-fall and tiny lake are still there — I have seen them." With that he stood up, shook Dad's hand, and walked into the night.

Dad pondered the story as he wrapped his blanket around him. He drifted off to sleep, dreaming of running effortlessly and silently along a forest path, until he came to a rushing stream high in the mountains, with elk grazing in a meadowy blanket of greens and blues, where not even the little Princess...nor The Son...nor The Wolf had yet disturbed their sanctuary.

THE LEGEND

His eyes watered from the piercing brightness of the midday sun, and his blanket lay on the ground, unneeded by his brown and supple torso in the summer heat. The Son, a young Indian boy of the beachcombers' village, had been on the bluff since early morning watching for his father, who might be returning today from his summer-long journey. Beside him on the bluff was the village tool-maker whose wrinkled brown hands worked over a basket of newly-wrapped fishhooks. The old man and the boy kept a circular vigil from their lookout, past the narrow line of cedar-planked lodges of their village to the north, out to sea, southward, and finally and briefly at the Olympic peaks on their right hand. They marvelled at the splotches of snow cradled between the peaks — they only knew of snow that came to their beach in rare winter storms and melted quickly. To see those snow fields shining in the summer sun was a mystery beyond their understanding.

This was the custom, to send one young and one old member of the tribe to the lookout, to watch for the dreaded war canoes of the fierce tribes to the north. The old toolmaker had seen them many times in his span of seventy years, and his fear was strong. The boy had only heard stories of the raiders from the shaky voices of the elders around the fires in the longhouse, and his only concern was for his father's return.

The Son's vigil had been faithful. Even when it was not his turn to be on the bluff, he had spent many hours watching the beach that stretched southward. He had expected his father to return two weeks ago from the Village-of-the-Hunter, where he had gone to learn their skill with the bow and arrow. The Son had been left in the care of the village Chief and his wife who took him into their lodge with their daughter, Whaht Kay (Fair Maiden). "The Little Princess" as the villagers had named her had become his close companion.

Now — there! a silhouette appeared far away. Blinking and shading his eyes, The Son could make out the figure of a man, but wait — there was a second figure beside him, a woman! His young heart pounded, and the momentary expectation he had felt now turned to confusion. If his father were bringing a woman home, it could mean only one thing — she would be his new mother.

The Toolmaker turned in surprise as The Son leaped and slid in angry strides down the side of the bluff, red dust and gravel flying behind him. He ran along the sand toward the village, calling the Princess. He must find her, and tell her about the woman — **he did not want a new mother!**

The Princess saw him coming, saw his troubled face, and heard the rambling words. Suddenly she was stumbling after him as he pulled her toward the beach where they could clearly see the approaching couple. The Son's hand tightened on hers. As she put her other hand on theirs, she recalled a sad time five years ago when The Son's mother had died from a strange, lengthy illness. The little boy had watched the men carry his mother's body to the Place-of-the-Dead near the edge of the forest, and place it on a platform well up in a tree, as was the custom of the village. It had been a dark moment for a child.

Now his father called to him, and they stood admiring the

2

strengths in each other — the older seeing the new signs of virility that he wished to see in his son, and the younger man seeing what he hoped to be — strong, tall, and confident in his manhood. He felt his father's hands on his shoulders as the words came at last, intruding upon the moment:

"This is your new mother, her name is Koba." The woman stared at her feet, so that neither The Son nor the crowd gathered around them could see her face. Someone laughed, and others mumbled to each other, making her more uncomfortable. The Son knew the name meant their phrase for **quiet** or the command to "shut up". He did not care — he needed no one to mother him. He was sure he could stay with the Chief for as long as he wished. Let his father and the woman have the lodge to themselves without him. During the past months he had thought about his future, planning to ask the Princess to marry him one day soon, and they would have their own lodge, their own life together.

Seeming to ignore The Son's indifference and brushing the woman aside, his father was showing off a wolfskin jacket and two fine bows and a bundle of arrows to the men. As for the jacket, he told how while hunting he had found a wolf which had been gored by an elk or deer, and had brought it back to the woman to make into the jacket. From that time on he was known as "The Wolf." He motioned to The Son to come now as they walked to their lodge. The Son went along reluctantly, taking time to whisper briefly to the Princess.

Restless to use his new skill, The Wolf spent more time hunting, leaving Koba in charge of his lodge. The boy and the woman were strangers — she was not like his mother, and the villagers did not seem to accept her. The Son continued to spend most of his time with the Princess and the other children, playing in the surf, gathering berries, and swimming in the stream. When The Wolf became aware of this incompatibility, he decided it would be good to take The Son with him on short hunts not far from the village. The Son learned to use the bow and liked the swiftness and power of the arrow. After the second trip he had become skillful enough to kill small game, rabbit or squirrel. Now The Wolf was determined to teach The Son to be his hunting partner.

One morning while The Wolf was on a longer trip, staying overnight in the forest, the boy awoke to find he was alone in the lodge —
Koba had left during the night to return to her people.

BEACHCOMBER TO HUNTER

At the time of this legend, "Wake   Iksum"—(long time ago), the first people who lived along the coast were mainly beachcombers. They were content to live out their years along the narrow corridor between the thundering surf on one hand and the dark timber on the other. They lived off the bounty provided by the sea —endless supply of oysters, clams, mussels, sea cucumbers, crab, smelt— and the salmon and trout that came up the neighboring stream to spawn.

They were not hunters, having few weapons of any kind. Winter storms sometimes forced the deer and elk down from the hills, and fierce wolves had been seen chasing them into the surf. The wolves, bear, and cougar did not molest the people, but they were feared by the villagers, enough that few of the men ventured into the forest.

Their lives followed a simple pattern of gathering food, making clothing, and other things necessary for mere survival. There were certain shells, stones, and bones that could be fashioned into cutting tools. The inner bark of the cedar, cherry, or maple could be made

5

into strips and woven into baskets, mats, clothing, and footgear. When storms would topple large fir or cedar trees, the masses of tiny rootlets were cut and made into cord, rope, or watertight containers.

The children, like all children, found time to run and play, especially on long summer evenings. Since this easy way of life was all they knew, they were content — except for one chilling threat: the raiders! Far to the north was the Village-of-the-War-Canoe. They were a war-like tribe who used big sea-going canoes to raid their more docile neighbors.

"They will take you away and make you slaves — you and the Princess, and your mother and father — everybody!" said one of the elders, sweeping his hand in their faces. "They can come at any time, and so fast there is no time to run — if you try to get away or fight them, they will kill you."

The elders talked often of past raids, but because this village was small, it had been passed over a long time; so long, in fact, that some of its young people had never experienced the terror of a raid, including the Princess and The Son who were now approaching their sixteenth birthdays.

During the years of his approaching manhood, The Son and The Wolf began to hunt daily. At first, they hunted small game nearby, but as their skills improved and their courage grew, they found their way deeper into the forest. The time came when they brought in their first deer. This called for a venison feast in the longhouse, with the villagers joining together in their admiration of the two hunters. Later, this became fairly common, providing a welcome change in diet, and the skins of the deer were useful for clothes, moccasins, water-carriers, and food storage.

The Son was pleased to be able to bring some special gift to his Princess, a portion of meat or an animal skin or fur. Their childhood friendship had grown into a deep love, and they began to plan for the time when they would have their own lodge.

Between hunting trips The Wolf worked to improve their hunting gear with the expert guidance of the Toolmaker. He lived with two other old men in the longhouse. In one corner of the house was his shop, where he used the slack-bow method to turn a spindle. With this tool he could drill holes in shells, bone, and wood by spinning a drill, using a splinter of very sharp stone for a point. He made excellent spears for salmon, and tiny hooks for trout and other fish. He shredded the inner bark of the wild cherry into tiny strips to secure sharp barbs on fishhooks and salmon spears. He was famous for his fire-making kits, which used a spindle to create fire by friction. The Wolf spent many hours with the old man, learning to make sharper arrowheads, arrows and stronger bow-strings.

CALL OF THE MOUNTAINS

The Wolf sometimes went up on the bluff where he would sit and gaze at the snowy mountain peaks far away beyond the tree tops. It seemed to him they called him to come there, and the more he studied their beauty, the stronger the call became. He found himself hunting alone more, as The Son was reluctant to spend time away from his beloved Princess.

To avoid having to spend cold, wet nights in the forest, The Wolf knew how to make shelters where he could have a fire and be warm and dry. His favorite shelter material was the thick heavy bark of a fir log, one that had lain on damp ground until its sapwood had rotted away. This left the bark free to be lifted in large pieces. It could easily be shaped by hand, and only a few pieces were needed to make a snug shelter. Smaller chunks were excellent long-burning fuel for a fire.

On his lone hunting trips The Wolf ventured farther and farther from the village. As these trips became longer, the old men muttered that someday he might not return.

"You take the fattest part of the venison from the bowl when he returns from the hunt with enough to feed you!" The old men were surprised to hear The Son speaking so boldly. One of the men spoke:

"I see that you eat well at the feast he brings home." The Son stood as straight as he could while the others looked at him.

"Some day the wolf or cougar will make a feast of him if he goes much farther into the forest." The Son turned and walked from the smoke-filled lodge, his eyes smarting with tears of anger — but secretly he feared they might be right.

The Wolf had lost his old fear of the forest and animals that made their home there. In his travels he had found some prairie-like openings in the timber, where only a few scattered trees grew in grassy areas. Such places were good hunting grounds, especially for deer. On his last trip he had found such a place, which was larger than any of the others he had seen. Making his way across he came upon a well-traveled game trail. He had found game trails before, but not as large and worn as this. After studying the tracks of the deer, elk, and bear, he decided to follow it. As it lead in the direction of those familiar mountains, he felt a new urgency to follow it.

In a short time the trail entered the dark timber, but The Wolf kept on until the trees gradually thinned out, and he saw more hardwoods and brush. As he came around a bend in the trail he stopped in his tracks. He just stood and stared at the strangest thing

10

he had ever seen, a little green valley where the stream, now much smaller, wound through meadows where deer and elk quietly fed. His wanderings had brought him at last to the foothills of the beckoning mountains.

Slowly he ventured out into the area for a better look. The deer and elk gave him one startled look and bounded away. A little farther out in the meadow he became aware of the mountain peaks above him. For some time he stood fascinated with the strangeness and beauty of his surroundings. The glaciers on the side of the mountains glistened in the sun, and while they seemed much nearer, he knew they were still a great distance away. He must go there soon, he thought.

He suddenly realized that the afternoon shadows were getting longer around him. It was time to find a place to spend the night. Not far off, in a bend of the stream he could see a grove of giant cedars and firs. There he found a large fir tree with thick, low-hanging branches — a ready-made shelter. Slipping off his pack, he placed it against the huge trunk of the tree. From his pack he took a special fire-making tool which the old Toolmaker had made for him and quickly built a fire. In a few minutes he had speared a trout with an arrow, bringing it back to the fire to broil for his evening meal. He thought about his discovery, and a feeling of excitement came over him. He could come here and live — and another idea; he must bring The Son to see this wonderful place.

Juice from the trout sputtered and hissed into the fire while he surveyed the area quickly. Nearby he found several big fir trees that had been blown down. They had lain there long enough to yield much of his favorite lodge-building material. After eating, he lay by the fire and watched a bright moon come up over the mountains. He lay drowsily listening to the little stream, but roused up quickly at the sound of a wolf far across the meadow. Another wolf answered from a short distance away. He wondered if they were talking about him, the stranger who had brought the first fire to their little valley. And did they know that he was wearing the skin of one of their brothers on his back? Gathering some night fuel, he lay down and slept.

When morning came he had a good meal, and set off exploring once more. Following the stream across the meadow, he discovered it came from a big pool at the base of a rocky cliff. After circling the valley, he returned to the big tree where he had spent the night. He was tempted to start building a lodge there, but he had been gone from the village a long time — it was time to return.

As usual he combined hunting with travel, and evening found him a long way from the beach with a storm coming. He raced along the trail to one of his shelters where he spent the night. In the morning, the storm had passed and he hurried on his way. It was mid-morning when he came out of the forest, and into the village.

He was not fully aware of the quietness, until he found his lodge empty. The people had vanished, leaving lodges and fires unattended. Running to the longhouse he found the villagers gathered there and in a state of panic. The Son stood before him.

"The war canoes from the north village came by this morning — we could see them beyond the breakers. There were four canoes full of warriors!" He was interrupted by the old Toolmaker, who said:

"They were looking us over very carefully — I don't trust them. They could come back at any time."

"We all ran for the forest, and they suddenly started paddling and moved on to the south. That was before midday. Some of our families are just coming back from the woods," said the Chief. After hearing their story, The Wolf told them about the beautiful valley he had seen, and how safe it would be from the threat of the raiders. He urged them to leave the village quickly. The Chief listened to The Wolf's description of the valley. He began a long, solemn speech, urging them to do as The Wolf suggested. Only a few of the younger men agreed that it was wise. Others spoke out of fear.

"We have always lived off the sea — it has been good to us."

"We are not forest people — there are dangerous things in the forest, and it is much colder there."

"There are evil spirits in the forest."

Seeing that their minds could not be changed, the Chief sent them back to their lodges.

12

"We will keep a better watch from the bluff —two men with sharp eyes, and no young boys, who fall asleep too easily after a day in the sun and wind." The Chief waved them out of the longhouse.

The Wolf and The Son then went to their lodge, where The Wolf tried to describe the little valley he had found. When he had finished, he told The Son of his dream — that The Son might return to the valley with him and help build a fine big lodge. The Son shook his head slowly:

"I cannot go now. I have asked Whaht Kay to marry me, and we will need to build a lodge of our own. I have been waiting to speak to you about this."

The Wolf was not surprised. He listened thoughtfully to his son. They sat talking quietly, each respecting the words of the other. There was a long, almost formal silence before The Wolf stood and placed his hands on The Son's shoulders:

"I think it is time, my son. I will give you and the Princess my lodge. If I go back to the valley and build a new lodge, I will be living there many weeks at a time, and when I come back to this place I will live at the longhouse with the old men." The Son could not speak. He knew what the lodge meant to The Wolf. It had been his home for many years, and The Wolf and his first mother had built it together. Then he heard The Wolf say:

"I will give you the lodge at sundown tonight." The Son felt love, gratitude, and pride welling up inside him as he answered:

"This is a fine thing you do. I will be proud to live here and care for this place as you have." Then he remembered the Princess. How excited she would be! He turned and ran to tell her and her parents the news, and soon all the village knew there was to be a ceremony that evening.

The raiders were forgotten.

13

THE CEREMONY

The whole village was caught up in the sudden preparations for the ceremony. There would be a feast, with gifts and special dress for the occasion. There was very little time before they were to gather at the lodge of the Chief.

And then it was time. The sky was slightly overcast, but not enough to hide the bright orb of the sun as it sank slowly toward the horizon. The Wolf and the Chief stood side by side, facing the sea. The Son and the Princess stood facing them, their backs to the sea. All was still except for the surf and the calling of the gulls.

The Chief made a little speech, telling the people what they already knew — that The Son and the Princess were going to live together in a lodge of their own. Now The Wolf stepped forward:

"When the lower edge of the sun touches the sea, my old lodge will belong to The Son." All except the happy couple watched the sun's descent. To the villagers it seemed to be suspended, immobile, and then they could see it was sinking. Just as the rim touched the

15

sea, The Wolf told The Son the lodge was now his and the Princess's. Then he stepped back and said no more. Lower and lower the sun dipped, and when half of it was below the horizon, the Chief announced that when it could not be seen, his Princess would belong to The Son of The Wolf. The Son then gave the Chief and the mother of the Princess a fine beaver skin each to seal the pact. Then the young couple turned around and walked a short distance toward the beach and stood watching as the sun disappeared. For a long moment one bright spot remained, and finally blinked out.

The Son and the Princess turned around and saw that they were alone — the people had stolen away quietly to wait for them in the longhouse. The Princess had seen this happen to other couples, and had dreamed of the day when it would happen to her. She fairly danced as she and The Son made their way to the longhouse where their friends greeted them with exciting chatter. Everyone, even the children had presents for them. The old Toolmaker had made the Princess a necklace of tiny dove shells. It was a proud moment for him when he saw how pleased she was, as she fastened it around her neck before many admiring eyes.

Food was plentiful, and the delicacies that came out of storage added to a pleasant time for all. When the feast had finally ended, the people melted away into the darkness, leaving The Wolf, the three old men, and the couple, who now made their way to their very own lodge. Someone had built a fire, and more gifts awaited them. At last they were alone to share a happiness beyond their fondest dreams.

The next morning there was no sign of the hated raiders, but the villagers were fearful of their return. Lookouts remained on the bluff. That afternoon the Chief and The Son took the Princess and her mother into the timber to a secret hiding place where the two women would go at the first sign of danger, to remain hidden until all danger was past.

The alarm rang out just two days later. The big canoes were coming back from the south. Once more the people panicked and ran into the forest to hide. The Chief, The Son and The Wolf remained behind at the edge of the forest. They had their bows ready and planned to retreat along the trail and kill any raiders that might follow them.

The faces of the warriors were visible now, their paddles paused in stride, and then unbelievably, they moved on toward their home village. When the Chief believed it was safe he sent word to the people to come home again, but it was a badly shaken band of people who ventured slowly back to their lodges.

In a few days, life in the village returned to normal. The men and women were caught up in their tasks, and the children played freely along the beach and streams. The happiest of all were The Son and his beloved Princess. The Princess realized that every day of her past life she had awakened to find her mother preparing the food for the coming day. Now it was her turn to do the same for her husband. Her happiness was complete.

The Wolf grew anxious to return to the valley, and wanted to start work on the new lodge. He expected that The Son would go with him, but when he spoke of it, The Son declined, promising to come later. He was still afraid of the raiders' return and unwilling to leave his Princess unprotected. Somewhat sad, The Wolf packed his tools and supplies and disappeared into the forest alone.

The days seemed to fly for The Son and his Princess. They did their daily tasks together in a spirit of fun. If he went to the head of the bay to spear salmon, she was beside him. They swam together in the bay and the surf, much as they had when they were children.

But a shadow began to fall on their happiness. The Son kept recalling his last sight of The Wolf going off alone. The promise he had made loomed larger each day until he decided he must leave the Princess and go after The Wolf. The Princess wanted to go with him, but he was reluctant to take her until he had been over the trail and was sure of the way. He was ready very early one morning, and they walked together toward the forest trail. After a tender embrace she asked:

"How many sunsets will come before you return?" Picking up a stick he drew one line in the sand.

"That is for one day to go there." Drawing three more lines, he said:

"These are the days I will be with The Wolf." Then he drew one

17

more line for the day it would take him to return, and with that he turned and left her standing alone. She looked down at the lines for a long time. For the first time since her marriage to The Son in the beautiful sunset ceremony, the Princess felt the beginnings of tears in

her eyes. But she held them back as she marked out the first line with her toe. Slowly she turned and went back to the village, to their lodge where they had been so happy.

"May Lala the Good Spirit bring you back safely," she said aloud. Her mother, hearing her prayer, looked up from her weaving to say softly:

"You will be going to the valley some day with him."

"We have never talked of it. I believed that we would always live here near the sea." Was her mother right? She was a quiet person, but very wise, and well-respected by all the women of the village.

"We should prepare for the time when you go beyond the forest to live." The older woman looked down at her work again and was silent. In the days that followed, the two of them began separating the dried fish and berries into smaller bundles for "the new lodge". Her mother made new clothes for her, which the Princess set aside, beginning to accept the idea that she would be going away. It would be good— she and The Son living in The Wolf's new lodge. The two hunters could be together again. She knew many ways she could be of help to the men, but best of all, she would be with her loved one.

THE RAID

The Princess had developed a ritual — each morning she built her fire, and before preparing any food she would hurry to the place where The Son had drawn the lines in the sand, and scratch one out. On the last day, she fairly flew there to erase the last line, thinking he would surely come as he had promised.

Today, however, as she turned back to their lodge again without him beside her, she began to doubt that he would ever come — she had lost count of the days since she had smoothed out the last line. As she neared the village, she could hear the happy shouts of the children playing on the beach. It reminded her of the times she and The Son had played there, and the memory cheered her for a moment.

Suddenly she realized that the playful noises had changed — they had become screams of terror.

"The canoes are coming! *raiders! raiders!*" The children had seen two large war canoes cutting through the surf, and after a quick look, they ran screaming the alarm through the village. She hesitated a moment, frightened and confused. But by now she could see the enemy faces — fierce looking — and they held clubs and spears in the air.

She remembered the secret hiding place, and turned and ran swiftly toward the woods, looking over her shoulder for her mother. There was no time to go after her, and now, terror-stricken, she crept beneath the thick brush and mass of vines. She dared not breathe, and lay trembling, hearing the screams of those captured by the raiders. Her mother did not come. Bewildered, she lay motionless, calling on Lala the Good One under her breath. Further screams, and she thought of how suddenly the carefree life of the village had come to an end.

The lookouts on the bluff must have been asleep. The warning had come too late for her mother to run away. The Chief tried to hide her in the driftwood, but they had been seen. When he tried to defend her, he was brutally slain in front of her eyes. The leader of the tribe pulled her from the driftwood and pushed her toward the line of villagers being led to the canoes. He had seen the Princess running into the timber.

"Bring that one to me — she will be my personal slave!" He waved his fist in the air and shouted at a tall, scar-faced man.

The lone warrior searched for the Princess, but could not find her. Now he was afraid for his own life — he knew very well the leader would be furious if he did not return with his prize, and he decided to look further.

His sharp eyes searched the ground for the tiniest sign of anyone's passing. Once he was so close to the Princess, she could her his loud breathing. She was sure he had found her, and she stifled a scream. Then he moved away. He had gone back down the trail to the beach. Still, the Princess was not certain he was not standing right over her, or waiting close by.

After a very long time, she raised up slowly until she could look around — he was gone!

"Oh, my husband, how much I need you now,'" she cried to herself as she crouched in the brush. Then she remembered: what if he

22

should return and be caught? She must warn him before he came back!

Cautiously she made her way to the trail, which out of fear very few of the villagers had ever taken. Now the thought of seeing her husband excited her so that she ran more swiftly into the forest. It was a tragic mistake!

Another raider had followed the trail, hoping to find more victims. Empty-handed, he was returning to the beach when, much to his surprise and delight, the little Princess came running around a bend in the trail, straight into his arms. The instant surprise and shock brought a scream from her throat, and she nearly fainted. But in the next instant, she was furiously battling with the brute, who could handle her as easily as a rag doll. His steel grip held her flailing arms to her sides.

"Let me go — let me *GO!*" she cried, but it was no use — she was a captive. He marched and dragged her back to the beach, where he proudly presented her to the leader, a cruel man. He seemed very pleased with her, and ordered her placed in his canoe, which was waiting to carry away half of the villagers. The rest of the captives were on another canoe, already making its way through the surf. The raid was over.

As they pushed her toward the beach, the Princess searched for her parents among the huddled villagers. They were not there. She consoled herself by hoping that they had either escaped or were on the other canoe. The outgoing tide had left the big craft resting on the sand, and the raiders now ordered the captives to help push it into the water. When it was finally afloat, they hurried the people aboard, and the leader gave orders to take the paddles and head the canoe out. Looking at the faces of her people — frightened and in shock — the Princess noticed that the raiders had brought the village's few children and three old men. The old men would be forced to help paddle the craft through the breakers as far as they could, but when they failed to suit the demands of their captors, they would be tossed into the sea. The children could be sold or traded, or kept as slaves for the raiders. The villagers had heard all these things from the old men of the village. Now the other men captives were ordered to help with the paddling and bailing, as water started coming in due to the heavy surf.

The Princess was treated as a special guest and sat amidships near the learder's command post.

"What is your name?" She realized he was standing over her and touching her hair. She trembled and turned her face away from his foul, fishy breath. His words exploded in her face:

"Tell me your *name*!" She felt her head being pulled back so that she had to look at him.

"Whaht K-k-k-ay." He let go of her hair and laughed proudly for all to hear.

"Whaht Kay! My fair maiden!" Some laughed, but most of the raiders seemed to fear any acknowledgement of the man's triumphant laughter. They turned to the task of moving the canoe out to sea, as their leader bellowed orders over them.

It was the first time the Princess or any of her people had been afloat on anything larger than the rafts they used for fishing in their little bay. When the Princess asked the villagers about her parents,

24

they just stared at her. They were frightened, and clung to each other for comfort as the canoe fought its way through the breakers. Shortly after passing the breakers, the sea flattened out, and big rollers lifted the canoe to the crest and slid it away, gliding down into the trough ahead of them.

Before they had gone very far, the Princess saw that the bow was being turned slowly to the north. Each time the craft crested, she would look back toward her home in the fading distance. In a very short time the beach was no longer visible, and the old bluff, which seemed like a mountain to the villagers, disappeared in the mist, far astern. Looking for the snowy peaks that had been visible from the bluff, she was astonished to see a whole row of mountains along the eastern horizon.

Another surprise awaited her — in all the confusion she had not noticed that her old friend, the Toolmaker was seated near her. She leaned over and called to him:

"My friend, have you seen my mother or father?" He did not reply at once. He was watching the warrior-leader, as he paddled in silence. She continued to watch his face, and once he seemed to mumble something about her mother. Was he trying to tell her that her mother and the Chief were on the other canoe?

"The leader, he watches us too carefully," he whispered to her finally. (In his youth, the old fellow had lived in a village where there were slaves, and he knew — too well — the sorry fate awaiting the Princess and the others. They would have to obey the slightest whim of their masters or be beaten or killed.)

The Princess was amazed at how smoothly the canoe moved through the water. A few times she caught a glimpse of the other canoe, but it was too far away for her to see or recognize anyone. The other two men from the longhouse were in the bow of her canoe. She could see that one of them was growing tired and leaned on his paddle. His hands were bleeding. (What a sudden change from our easy way of life, thought the Princess.)

"Ah-eee-yiii-i" came the old man's cry, and she was startled to see the leader pick him up from where he had collapsed at his post, and toss hm overboard. The captives were stunned – they had never

25

seen anything so cruel — they could not believe what had happened. The Princess wept softly as did many of the women. But within the hour they were to witness the same fate for the second old man.

Through her tears, the Princess saw the leader climbing over the people toward her friend, the Toolmaker. The old man was pretty clever, and had been studying the situation closely. He rested just enough to conserve his strength and still appear to be paddling as he should. The raider stood over him for a minute and then moved back to his post. For the first time in her life the Princess felt **hate**. She realized she hated those who could be so cruel to her people.

Looking at the sun, she knew the time was approaching mid-day. It seemed that they had been sailing much longer. Now, in addition to their other miseries, the captives had become seasick. The raider had both food and water for his men, but gave none to the captives. As the big canoe moved on its way, they began to see more driftwood in the water. There must have been a fierce storm in the northern ocean, for trees and logs had been loosed into the water around them.

The Princess tried not to look at the Toolmaker, but could not help notice that he grew weaker, and she was afraid now for his life. Her fears were well founded, but she had underestimated the old man's ability to look out for himself. The leader had been watching him, but turned away for a moment. In that moment the Toolmaker gave her a quick smile, and in one motion rose up and leaped over the side, taking the cedar paddle with him.

When the leader saw what had happened, he was furious that the old fellow had outwitted him, but there was nothing he could do about it — the canoe was coasting down one side of a big wave while the Toolmaker was on the opposite side and floating toward shore.

("Oh, Lala, Good Spirit, help him make it to shore,") she prayed. She was thinking that if he got to shore he could go back to the village and tell The Son what had happened to her. But then, what could The Son do? He would not know where to find her. She tried to picture him at their lodge, but her mind was in a whirl. The canoe pushed northward with its cargo of frightened and ill captives.

By mid-afternoon the leader was watching the mountains to the

26

east very closely. This was his way of calculating the progress of the canoe. The Princess could see he was looking at a big headland, which began to loom large ahead of them. Later she could more accurately judge its size as it reached out into the sea. She became aware that if they kept on their present course, they would pass it before nightfall, and this worried her. Something told her that once they passed the headland, she might not be able to find her way back, nor would The Son be able to find her in this new territory. Her spirits were very low at the thought of never seeing her husband again.

Through the clouds to the west she noticed the long day was coming to a close. As a huge wave lifted the canoe high, she saw the headland clearly. The trees on the highest point were still in bright sunlight, but farther down, dark shadows began to lengthen. Thinking about the old Toolmaker, she was glad that he had gone overboard before they passed this point of land — she felt he was safely on his way back to the village.

Suddenly the leader stood up and signalled to the other canoe which had come up behind them and was now on their seaward side. The Princess tried to get a good look at it, hoping to see her family, but it was gone after only a glimpse. She watched eagerly for another chance, but it was not to be, the great walls of water separating them from view.

Another big wave pitched them high, and as they slid down the trough, the canoe gave a violent shudder and stopped dead in the water. They had run onto a deep-floating driftlog, and the bow of the canoe was well on top of it. The raiders knew instantly what had happened, and the leader took command of the situation.

"You — over the side," and he pushed two men overboard to stand on the log and push the canoe free. They struggled but could not move it. The leader sent two more men over to help, and moved some of the captives back amidships to lighten the load on the bow. The men shoved and groaned in the rough sea, but the canoe would not budge.

Shouting words of fury at the men, the leader turned to look shoreward, to the line of relentless breakers. He knew that once in the grip of those powerful waves, the log would shatter the canoe to pieces. To make matters worse, the paddlers were losing control, and the canoe was turning broadside to the oncoming waves. Darkness also threatened.

"Push, push!" the leader screamed, standing right next to the Princess. The men, unable to maintain a steady foothold in the rough sea, were exhausted — they were no match for the huge log which held them in place. In the dimming light the Princess saw that one of the four men on the log was the big warrior who had captured her that morning.

She saw something else that seemed unimportant at the time. The far end of the log was a mass of roots, some extending far above the water. The sound of the breakers grew louder and closer. The leader shouted more orders, just as an oncoming wave caught the root-mass and swung the log sharply about, twisting it free from the canoe.

"Turn, turn — take us out of here," raged the leader, and as they turned he fell on top of her, the smell of his body repulsing her. "That way, *that* way," he yelled as he climbed over the people and into the bow. The four men on the log were scrambling to get back aboard. Three of them made it, but the fourth made a desperate leap and fell into the water. The canoe pulled away, leaving him floundering and shouting after them.

Unconcerned for the life of one man, the leader shifted the captives toward the bow again. Suddenly — something was wrong — **the Princess, his prize captive was gone**. He had been too busy to notice until now. He threatened the paddlers who had been near her for allowing her to escape. He jerked a paddle from their hands and beat them on the head and shoulders as he searched the surrounding waters. but she was gone.

In the confusion of trying to free the canoe, the Princess had seen the tangle of roots come sweeping close by. For an instant the idea to slip over the side flashed through her mind, and then, without hesitating she obeyed the impulse. In a twinkling she was swimming the few strokes needed to reach the log. Getting a firm grip on a section of roots, she pulled herself up among them, and hung there above the water. Afraid of being pursued, she turned to look at the canoe, but it

28

was gone — she barely saw the stern as it slid away over a wave.

If she felt any relief in escaping the raiders, it was only momentary, for there, standing on the far end of the log, waving his arms wildly was the man who had captured her earlier. He was calling to the vanishing canoe. As she glanced at him, a sudden turn of the log caused him to fall, and he lay grasping a short broken limb, and glaring at her. An instant later, the ugly face disappeared beneath a wave. Lips trembling from the cold she murmured a prayer of thanks.

Looking shoreward, the Princess clung to the big log as it entered the breakers, not far now from the big headland. The point resembled the prow of a mighty ship, as it parted the oncoming waves and sent them swirling along the rocky beaches on either side. This added to the turbulence which the log and its rider had to pass through if the Princess were to survive. Now there was only one thing for her to do — try to cling to the big log as long as possible.

Actually the log was an enormous fir tree, with much of its top and branches intact. This, and the fact that it was riding toward shore at right angles to the waves, reduced its tendency to roll. She was riding high, and although the waves drenched her, she was able to take a breath between drenchings. The farther the log moved into the turbulence, the rougher the ride. Cross-currents began to turn the log broadside to the waves, rolling it from side to side and pulling her under at the end of each roll. Once a big wave pushed her — down, down, and **down** — until she thought she was to drown finally in the blackness, but at last the rolling motion brought her up to catch a precious gulp of air.

It seemed to her that the log would never pass through the waves, but gradually the buffeting became less violent, and each roll more gentle.

"Lala the Good One, you have been with me," she thought. It had been a fearful, battering ride through the waves, and it was difficult to comprehend that she had survived. As for the big warrior, the waves must have taken him under, but the fear that he might still be out there lingered in her mind.

THE LONG SWIM

She could see the dark mass of land towering above her as she rode along more smoothly now. A white line began to show through the darkness to her left, where the surf crashed against the rocks on shore. Her instincts told her that somewhere up ahead the beach must curve to the south toward her home, the old village. There she was sure The Son or The Wolf was waiting for her!

She hoped the log would carry her to the beach before the tide turned around and took her back into the wild sea. Her clothes clung to her cold, wet body, and she was weak from hunger. It had been one very long day and night since she had eaten or tasted fresh water. Weary, she sensed the log beginning to slow down. That meant the tide would be approaching flood stage, and she peered ahead, hoping to see some sign of the beach where she might get to shore.

Occasionally there would be a break in the overcast, which would let some moonlight through, but otherwise the night was getting darker. When the next light broke through, the white surf line

31

was still on her left. The light also revealed a group of logs that had gone aground a few yards from shore, but too far away for her to swim to them. In her present condition she could not hope to swim that far. While looking desperately for some chance to get ashore, she was terrified to hear;

"Oh-h-h, help," and then coughing and moaning coming from the far end of the log — **the big raider was still with her!** Now she had to find a way to escape, but how? The tide was barely moving the water around her. Suddenly the moonlight was gone and she could see nothing. The sounds from the end of the log grew louder. Another flash of moonlight showed an object like a tiny island in the shadows ahead. Climbing down to the water's edge, she was determined to swim to it or die trying. As she came nearer, she saw that it was just the end of a big log fast aground.

Slipping into the water, she swam a few floundering strokes and caught a firm hold on the log. Clinging to it with her head barely above water, she lay motionless while the log that had been her means of escape from the canoe drifted slowly by. As it came close to her, the big raider was within an arm's length, **but he did not see her.** When she could see him no more, she used her last bit of strength to pull herself up and onto the top of the log. She was too exhausted to try to swim to the beach. She slumped down, wet and shivering, while the sounds of the raider faded away into the night. And miraculously, despite all her discomfort, she dozed off.

The Princess did not know how long she had slept when she was awakened by a **thump, thump** — there it was again! Something nudged her log. The moon was bright, and there — floating with one end against her log was the other log with the raider on it. The tide had brought him back! Fear of his face, his grip — all those terrible memories flashed before her eyes — as she measured the distance to the beach, determined to slip beneath the water if he tried to reach her.

She watched breathlessly as he tried to get to his feet, but a cloud suddenly shut out the light, and it was impossible to see him clearly. Her heart pounded wildly when the light once again revealed him standing up and looking in her direction. She could see the tide was pulling the log just slightly away. He started to move toward her. 'No, no!' she thought, when a violent spasm of coughing seized him and he went down on his hands and knees. The tide drew the log away faster now, and as she huddled low, barely breathing, the log and her enemy drifted away toward the waves which crashed in the distance. Now she was free of him, but too miserable to fully realize it. After a long time she fell asleep again, lost in a deep, total sleep.

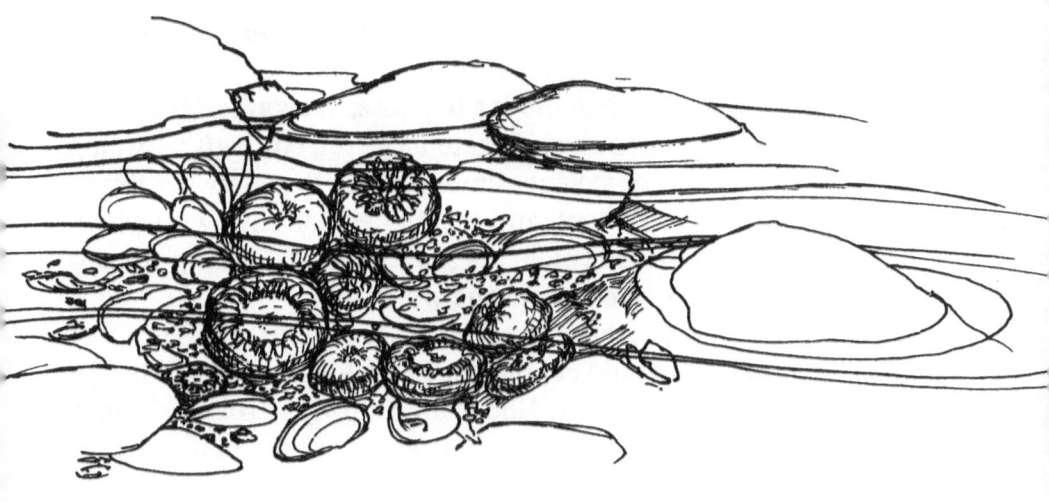

HOME!

Bright sunlight awakened the Princess the next day. The side of her
body facing the sun was warm and dry. During her first waking
moments she began to recall events of the night and how she came to
be there. She felt stiff and bruised, her arms and legs scratched raw in
places. She put her hands to her face, and then her hair, stiffened
from the salt water. Not until she tried to stand up on the log did she
realize how weak she was — and so very hungry.

The tide was at low ebb, and her log stretched away over a
muddy cove to the gravel beach. In the tidal pool alongside the log
she could see crab and other shellfish, and she knew there would be
oysters on the rocks ashore.

"The canoe — the raider", she said aloud; she suddenly remembered all the terror of the night before with disturbing freshness. She
looked in all directions about her, afraid they would come out of
nowhere to take her away. But there was no one, only the familiar
sounds of the beach — the swish, swish of the waves, the faint crack-

ling of dry seaweed — to remind her of her life in the little village. (Her village; perhaps gone forever?)

After a shaky walk along the log to shore, she gathered enough shellfish for a feast. When she had eaten, she felt strength returning to her legs, and walked to a clear-running brook to satisfy her thirst. The water was cold and sweet, and she dipped handfuls with which to wash her face and the cuts on her legs and arms. Climbing up onto some driftwood, she sat resting in the warm sun.

She had but one thought now, to be on her way to the village. She had no idea how far it would be, but she had a feeling it would not be an impossible distance for her. She waded slowly across a shallow cove and climbed to the sandy beach, from where she could see the sand stretching away toward the west, **not** southward as she had hoped.

The Princess and her people had never understood how to review the problems and factors affecting their daily lives in a systematic, rational way. They made decisions from habit and instinctive urgings from their subconscious. Now as she sat resting she was dimly aware of the fact that the series of savage events beginning with the raid had somehow begun to change for the better. She had escaped from the raiders' canoe, and had watched the hated warrior drift away into the night, two things in her favor.

"Lala-the-Good-One was with me", she told the sandpipers strutting along the water's edge. Was it Ogoo-the-Evil-One who had brought about the loss of her mother and the Chief? She had known very little evil in her young life, and feared even to acknowledge his presence. The old men in the longhouse spoke of the daily contest between Lala and Ogoo.

"You cannot see these spirits — they are invisible. But they are at war all around us." She recalled now the warning of the old men, and how a chill had gone through her as she heard the words while the firelight flickered across the Toolmaker's face when he spoke.

"May the Good One be stronger than the Evil One," she prayed, "and bring The Son back to me."

Dreams of their reunion, the feeling of his arms about her filled her thoughts, and she did not realize that she approached the point where the beach now curved southward. Excited, she peered into the distance, hoping to see the old bluff. It could not be too far, although her estimate of how far she had travelled in the canoe was vague. She tired easily, and finding more shellfish, she chose a sunny perch in the driftwood where she could eat and rest briefly.

From long experience she kept a sharp eye on the edge of the surf, looking for objects swept ashore with the tide. She walked close to the surf for two reasons: the sand was firmer and easier for walking, and the waves washed away her footprints. Weary again, she was about to stop and rest when she saw the sun glistening on something in the little wavelets. She ran through the water, kicking spray ahead of her.

"The paddle — the Toolmaker's paddle!" It had to be the paddle her friend had taken with him when he leaped from the canoe. What if he had made it ashore! She called out several times, and searched the area for signs of him, but there was only the paddle, which she carried into the driftwood, to sit and ponder about her friend. He was much older than she, and she had needed all of her young strength to survive the ocean. Had he chosen to drown of his own choice, rather than be enslaved or killed by the raiders? Or would she still find him along the beach or in the village? She called him again, her voice lost finally in the wind and cry of the sea birds.

Time to move on. She carried the paddle, leaning on it whenever she stopped to look behind her to see if she were being followed. The headland faded smaller and smaller behind her in the distant mist. The day had been beautiful, but now as the afternoon grew late, clouds gave notice of a threatening storm. Out at sea a big rain squall headed for the land ahead of her. She was very tired now, and wished that she might see the familiar old bluff in the distance.

She came to another small stream, and as she poked about for crayfish, she was suddenly aware she had been here before, **many times!** Now she knew where she was — the village was not far. She ran eagerly in spite of her weakness, more excited each time she recognized a familiar landmark.

The rains came and drenched her, but she paid little attention. The joy of finding the familiar little creek was not enough to keep her tired legs moving. The storm had passed but had left her cold and shivering.

"It can't be too far — why is it taking so long for me to get there?" she asked herself. She stumbled over a log, and sank down on the beach. And then, over the booming sound of the surf, she thought she could hear running water — she could not be sure — she had been disappointed so many times before that she doubted her judgement. Getting to her feet, she walked a few paces, and found she was standing in the familiar stream of her village — **she was home!**.

Scrambling and splashing up out of the stream, she ran and stumbled toward the village, calling loudly for The Son. There was no answer. As she ran toward the lodge, her hopes for a joyous re-union turned to fear. Still calling, she made her way to the lodge and found it dark and silent — painfully silent. Disappointed and with a heavy heart, the little Princess sank to the ground and began to weep.

Thoughts of The Son, or instinct for survival — perhaps both factors forced the Princess, cold and forlorn, to rouse herself and find materials for a fire, which she methodically started. The first licks of firelight showed the lodge to be just as she had left it the morning of the raid. The raiders had not come here, or had been more eager to carry away people then possessions. She could tell that The Son had not returned from the valley with The Wolf. If he had, there would have been some sign of his living there, but she knew nothing had been changed.

For the Princess, this was the first day in her life when she had been all alone. It was hard for her to believe that there was no other person in her friendly village. Here was where she had been born, and given the name Whaht Kay, had learned to walk and play with the other children, and where The Wolf had presented the lodge to her and The Son in that ceremony at sunset — all had been so good before the raid.

Not until she had taken a fire-brand from her fire and gone to the longhouse, and looked quickly into the Chief's empty lodge, did she begin to understand the bitter truth — the villagers, her parents, The Wolf, and her loved one — all were **gone**! Confused and utterly

38

exhausted, she built up the fire and lay down beside it, listening to another rainstorm approaching in the fading afternoon.

In a little while her clothes began to dry, and she felt warmth returning to her body. There was plenty of smoked fish hanging above the fire. She took some down and prepared a good supper, before falling asleep. Sometime during the night she was awakened by terrible dreams of the raiders. So real were the dreams that she sat up, ready to run, and then lay down again, listening and expecting to hear them coming after her. Then the rhythmic pounding of the waves on the beach began to calm her, and before the first dim rays of daylight, she fell asleep once more. This time no dreams disturbed her, and she slept well into the morning.

When she awoke the sun was shining from a blue, cloudless sky. After a brief moment of fearful recollection, and a quick search of the area, she nursed the fire alive and prepared her breakfast.
"How I wish he would come today—to share this breakfast with me. Maybe he will return today, maybe today." Her thoughts were filled with hope once more.

TEARS IN THE SAND

It seemed to the Princess that her clothes had become tainted with the mere presence of the raiders. She tore them off and went to the little bay and bathed. She ran back to the lodge to dry herself by the fire, and put on the new clothes her mother had helped her make for the trip to the new lodge — 'someday soon', her mother had said as she sewed by the fire.

The bath, the new clothes, and familiar surroundings — she felt refreshed and excited, for the first time since that awful morning. Hurrying to the place where The Son had drawn the lines in the sand, she redrew them all. Then she added two more, one for the day she had spent walking down the beach, and another for the present day. Now she could see that The Son had stayed only two days longer than he had said — surely he would come back soon.

Unaware of another shocking experience awaiting her, she walked slowly back to the lodge. Although the deserted village was a dismal sight, she could not resist the urge to walk through it, half

41

expecting to see some of the happy faces, and hear the sounds she knew.

It was difficult for her to enter the Chief's lodge, her former home, but she went in and looked about at the familiar signs of her past. She found her mother's sewing tools — bone needles and an awl which the Toolmaker had made for her — just as the mother had left them. Taking the sewing basket and some clothing with her, she stepped into the sunlight facing the ocean. As she studied the seascape ahead, something strange in the foreground of her vision seemed to beg for attention. There was an unnatural formation in the driftwood.

She walked slowly toward the object. It was a body, a light veil of sand covering the shape. And then she looked closer, and saw... it was the body of the Chief, her father, lying where the raiders had killed him.

What a terrible discovery! The Princess was overcome with shock and grief. Her knees turned to water beneath her, and she fainted. The hard, cool sand rose up to meet her, and she lay motionless for a few seconds. She regained consciousness, slowly taking in the reality of the moment. She began to sob uncontrollably. For a long time she lay in shock, but finally forced herself to stand and walk to the lodge.

She needed a large basket, which she found and took back to the place where her father had fallen. Scooping up sand, she covered his body —there was no way she could take him to the Place-of-the-Dead. When her sad task was finished, she knelt and wept again, with only the gulls to hear her.

If ever she needed the comfort of her loved one, it was then, but he was not here. The fading afternoon turned to dusk, and the Princess forced herself to keep a fire going, but was otherwise numb to her surroundings. Darkness came as she lay staring into the flames, trying to comprehend how the gentle, easy-going life of her village could be so abruptly and savagely changed. Despite the hope that The Son would return, the heartache of losing her parents caused the tears to flow. Once or twice she left the lodge to look toward the trail head, but her eyes could not focus in the failing light, and she turned back to the shelter of the lodge.

Too many days had passed now, and she erased all the lines she had drawn in the sand, and drew no more. She could not remember just when she had given up her vigil, but she was growing more certain that The Son and The Wolf were gone, just as all the others. She had not heard another voice for so long that she imagined them, day and night. One day, when all her sorrow and loneliness seemed to combine to make her life in the village unbearable, she went to the bluff, where she could look north and south, hoping something would tell her where to go or what to do.

Once more she looked to the place where the trail emerged from the forest — that was where she had last seen him. A strong instinct told her that he was out there somewhere, and that being her strongest feeling at the moment, she was tempted to start up the trail. By the time she had come down from the bluff, she was determined to make the journey to the valley.

SAFE IN THE VALLEY

Recalling how hungry she had become during the past days' horror, the Princess took several fish from their drying rack, and wrapped a shell-full of dried berries in deerskin, and put them in her small pack with a fire-tool.

"I will not be afraid of the darkness — I must find him!" she told herself, as she started for the trail. It was a brave start, but when she came to the bend in the path where the hateful, foul-smelling warrior had swept her into his arms, she stood frozen in her tracks; she could not move. The scene came back to mind with all its stark terror; she turned around and ran back to the village.

She sat down in the lodge, confused and depressed by the lonely surroundings. It was then that the basket in the corner attracted her attention. It had been left there by The Wolf when he moved out. She recalled that The Wolf's strange woman, Koba had made it.

The Princess picked up the basket, and as she turned it slowly in her hands, the memory of the woman came alive, as if she were standing there. Her mother had liked Koba and had felt sorry for her, being a stranger and rejected by The Son. In her imagination, the Princess heard the woman calling her, and she felt drawn to her. She knew that Koba had come from the village to the south, and while the Princess had never been there, she was sure she could find it. She became more excited as she thought about it, this strange feeling being all the motive she needed to act. With one last look toward the trail, she turned and began her impulsive journey to the village of Koba, the woman who was to have been The Son's new mother...

...When the old Wolf left the village alone the last time, just before the raid, he was impatient to get back to the beautiful valley he had found. The heavy pack he carried slowed him down, and night found him far from his destination. 'Maybe I'm growing old', he thought. He spent the night in one of the shelters he and The Son had used many times. The next morning he made an early start and arrived at the big fir tree by mid-day. A smile crinkled his eyes as he walked around and around the tree — 'it is perfect!' he said aloud.

He immediately began building the lodge. First, he selected dead and well-seasoned fir poles from timber nearby for the framework — they would support the heavy chunks of thick fir bark. With a roaring fire he burned off the roots and tops to get the proper lengths. The large low-hanging limb would be used for a ridge-pole, and the huge trunk of the tree would serve as an end wall. The lodge began to take shape, and The Wolf was very pleased with his work, but suddenly realized that he felt strange — weak and feverish. By the next evening he could barely feed himself and keep his fire going.

It was then that The Son came and found him. The Wolf was so weak that he could only whisper directions to The Son for finding the herbs he knew would help him. After a few minutes' searching The Son found the herbs, and using some large seashells, he brewed two kinds of hot tea. With a smaller shell for a spoon he was able to get The Wolf to sip a little of the hot liquids. After two days, The Wolf seemed to be recovering, but he was still very weak.

The Son found himself very involved with care of The Wolf, but continued work on the lodge, following the instructions of his father.

He was anxious to return to the village for the Princess. He knew he had been gone much longer than he had promised. Each time he was about to leave, it seemed that The Wolf needed him more.

One morning The Son caught three small salmon, which he prepared for their evening meal, and he and The Wolf feasted on them. The older man improved daily now, even helping for short periods on the lodge. With the lodge nearly finished, The Son moved their gear into it, and leaving food and plenty of fuel at hand for The Wolf's comfort, he set out for the beach, promising to return within three days.

He left at first daylight and traveled faster than he ever had. At mid-afternoon he came running out of the forest, calling:

"Whaht Kay, Whaht Kay — I'm home." As he neared the lodge, he expected to see her coming to meet him, and was puzzled when she did not answer — and then alarmed when he found the lodge empty. Outside, the stillness surrounded, pressed in upon him. The lodges and longhouse were intact, and he ran to the empty longhouse, to the lodge of the Chief, still calling the Princess. His anxiety gave way to cold understanding — **the raiders had come!**

Suddenly he remembered the hiding place that he and the Chief had prepared. He found it, and saw that it had been used, but could find no signs of a struggle. He turned and ran back to the village, his thoughts tumbling in disbelief and fear for his loved ones. At the lodge he built a fire, and then ran to the top of the bluff and scanned the beaches as far as he could see. There was nothing, no one to explain what had happened. The long stretches of sand were deserted. He climbed down and walked through the village again. The tracks in the sand were many days old. (Even the tracks the Princess had made that morning were filled with blown sand, and the tide had washed away her footprints leading away from the village.)

'Where can she be — did the raiders take everyone?' he tortured himself with questions, and with the guilt he felt for leaving the village when he did. He was very tired but felt he must keep looking for her. Evening closed around him as he went once more, searching and calling into the empty night. The only answer came from the gulls and the pounding waves. At last, he returned to the lodge —

47

their lodge, where they had been so happy, and spent a long, lonely night.

When he awoke the next morning, he immediately resumed his search, trying to piece together the story of the raid. Although he found evidence of violence around the village, there were no clues to the Princess' disappearance. (Somehow The Son passed by the sandy mound where the Princess had covered her father's body.) Why had he stayed away so long, or even left her alone, he agonized over and over. If only he had stayed with her, he might have saved her. Defeated, he gave up the search, and not wanting to spend another lonely night where they had once lived together, he took his pack and began his journey back to the valley...)

...The lonely Princess made her way down the beach, which seemed to ramble on forever. Her only companions were the gulls flying overhead, and little colonies of cheerful sandpipers, fluttering across the surf ahead of her. By mid-afternoon she began to tire, and wondered how much farther it might be to the village. She squinted ahead for some sign of smoke curling against the sky. When evening came and still no signs of life, she unrolled her mat of cedar bark and took shelter behind a big log. She had no way of knowing that at that very moment, The Son was running through her village, calling her name.

Her enthusiasm for the journey to Koba's village began to fade — her instincts were muddled and the walking tiresome. To add to the turmoil within her, she was to have a bad experience the next afternoon when two rough-looking men resembling the raiders came along the beach and stopped to look toward her hiding place in the drift. They started in her direction twice, but finally turned and left, thinking perhaps that her tracks were of their own people. They moved on toward the south.

Very cautiously the Princess turned around to retrace her steps toward her home village, moving carefully during the two days, and hiding well during the night.

It was moonlight when she stepped into the empty lodge and started to build a fire. But what was this? The firepit was **warm**! A fire had burned out just a short time ago. Her first thought was the **raiders** — they **had** come back for her. Slipping outside she stood listening and peering into the shadows. There was no sound other than the beach sounds, and she returned to the shelter of the lodge and slept once more, alone.

When morning came, she could hear the wavelets lapping close by. The daylight brought a delightful surprise: there was fresh firewood placed as only The Son would have left it. He had been **there**! She was dazed by the thought that he had come back for her and she had not been there. Disappointed and confused, she sat huddled in the lodge into the late morning hours, dreaming of being with him again. Later, she went out and followed his tracks where he had searched for her, and then they led into the forest — he had gone back to The Wolf. She knew she would have to follow him there, and she began making plans for the journey.

It had been midsummer when the raiders attacked the peaceful beach village. Now green huckleberries appeared on the bushes along the stream, a sign of summer's end approaching. It also signalled the coming of the salmon, and many stirred the surface of the bay and stream. The Princess speared and smoked the few she would need for food on the trip to the valley. This delayed her plans to follow The Son, but not for long. One evening she knew she was ready to leave with the first light of dawn.

When the morning sun played through the cracks of the lodge wall, she was anxious to get started and determined that she could overcome the fears of the trail. After breakfast she was about to leave, and took one last look at the beach for signs of the raiders, and was frightened to see **people** walking down the beach from the north! The deadly terror of the raid seized her again, and she panicked and ran into the driftwood to hide. Then she remembered her pack — she had left it inside the lodge, but it was too late to retrieve it now.

As the strangers came closer, she could see a man, woman, and two children. They reached the lodge, and the woman and children stopped. The man had seen the smoke and he looked inside. In a moment, he came out, and after looking around he called to the others to come. To the Princess they looked just like her people, and her fear began to fade. The woman reminded her of her mother, and she could not resist the urge to go to her.

Hardly aware of her actions, she came out of hiding and smiled at the woman, and her smile was returned. Suddenly they were all talking and acting like a family who had just been reunited. It was the first human voice the Princess had heard since the day of the raid, and she was elated and warmed by their friendliness.

"The raiders — they come here, too?" They looked about them. "They kill many of our families, take our spears and food. We hide under an old canoe buried in the sand — they walk right over us."

"My... my father is buried over there, and I don't know where my mother is," said the Princess and began to cry. The woman came to her and held her until her tears had stopped. The Princess led them to her old home, the lodge of the Chief, and told them to make their home there. The little family thanked her in grateful tones, and the two little girls jumped up and down and ran to find their sleeping places.

"Will you not stay with us here — we will care for each other."

"No — I must be on the trail soon to find my husband — we had only been married a little while before the raid. I am sure he has gone to the valley near the mountains. He is a hunter, and finds much game there." The man looked up from his unpacking.

"I, too, am hunter." This was the most she heard from him — he seemed quiet, bitter perhaps from his experience with the raiders.

She was to see him on the bluff many times the next few days looking for some sign of the enemy.

The coming of the strangers had delayed the Princess, but she enjoyed being with them, to hear words, see a smile, and have strong arms embrace her at times. The father began working on a spear for her when he realized that she intended to make her journey to the valley. He showed her how to use it for defense if need arose, and how it could be used for a walking stick.

The mother did not want her to leave, and tried to find excuses to keep her with them. They had become like a family. The father brought in small game just as The Wolf and The Son had done. The

taste of the roast game in her mouth brought back the memory of those times when her loved one had returned with food for their table, and she thought of him in every waking moment. Early one morning, she rolled up her mat and announced that she was leaving. They all followed her to the trail, where The Son had left the Princess. There were a few tears in the parting with the family, and the father touched the spear he had made for her and said:

"No need to be afraid of forest — this spear will protect you." Feeling very brave, the Princess turned away from them and ran up the trail, her heart beating hard as she passed the terrible place where she had been captured.

The trail hugged the stream most of the way, its sounds a comfort to the Princess. She could not travel as fast as a man, but she kept a steady pace. Occasional openings in the forest canopy overhead told her where the sun was, and when it was directly overhead, she felt she had come a long way. In places the stream curved away from the trail, forcing her to walk in darkness; the stillness frightened her. She was not aware of it, but it was the first time in her life that she could not hear the sounds of the surf. She had seldom worn moccasins on the beach, and here they seemed to make loud noises as she hurried through twigs and leaves in the shadows.

And then — at a muddy creek crossing — **she saw The Son's tracks**, giving her new courage to walk faster, closer now to the time when she would see him again.

At mid-afternoon she came to one of The Wolf's shelters. Hungry and tired she stopped to eat and rest. The temptation to stay there overnight was strong, but the drive to keep going was even stronger. It seemed like a long distance before that she came to a place where the stream turned sharply away from the trail. It led through perhaps the darkest places she had yet seen, with giant evergreens rising skyward, their thick branches overlapping to blot out the sun. Strange sounds seemed to come from the depths of the forest on each side, and gripping her spear, she moved bravely along until the timber thinned out into a grassy opening.

The sudden change from darkness to light was exciting — could this be the Wolf's little valley? It was soon evident that it was not, as

52

another patch of forest awaited her. Following the trail through the grass had been easy compared to the blackness of the forest trail. She was to find other such areas but none fitting The Wolf's description of the beautiful valley carpeted with lupine and lilies, rippling grasses and game trails. The unusual effort of the journey was tiring her, and she hoped that soon she would come upon another shelter where she might rest in safety.

A glance toward the sun showed it would soon be slipping behind the timber to the west. This meant night was not far off, and the thought of being alone in the forest terrified her. Instinctively she looked for the stream off to her right. Wearily she made her way through the brush until she could hear the rushing water, and she stumbled onto the bank. She was pleased to see that it divided around a small, pine-covered island. Wading across she prepared camp for the night. There was plenty of wood at hand, so she built a fire and broke off a few pine boughs with which to make a shelter close to the fire. The fish she carried made a good meal, which she ate as the sun disappeared.

Despite her weariness, the warmth of the fire, and the soothing sounds of the stream on each side of her, sleep did not come easily. It was the first time in her life she would be without the surf sounds for a lullaby. Resting under the shelter she began to doze off, dreaming of The Son and hoping to be with him before another night passed.

"Owww-oooo-ooo'" — the piercing howl of a wolf woke her. Listening carefully, she heard the sounds of running deer, and momentarily saw the yellow flicks of fire reflecting in their eyes. Then the noises ceased and she fell asleep again. Later, she was awakened by sounds of splashing, and she raised up to see more bright eyes, as a family of raccoon stood watching the stranger on their island.

Morning brought storm clouds hurrying across the sky. She built up a fire for her breakfast, wondering if she were still being watched by her night visitors. Feeling refreshed, she shouldered her pack and waded ashore, eager to be on her way to the valley.

The next stretch of timber did not seem as large as the others she had passed the day before, and she soon came to another grassy area.

Before she reached the other side of the little meadow, she came upon a game trail, and in the mud she saw a man's tracks — The Son's! There was no doubt about it, and she knew that the valley must be close now. The trail lengthened out through more forest, but she hurried along, her moccasins fairly dancing over the twigs and leaves. Brush caught at her hair, and she noticed more hardwood trees. Then it began to rain. She ran now, and as she came around a bend, a lovely sight opened up before her — there was the valley — and the lodge waiting for her.!

She ran toward the big shelter, recognizing the work of The Wolf. She called loudly as she approached the lodge, expecting to see her loved one coming to meet her. Her calls went unanswered. A cold fear filled her as she reached the entrance.

Clumsily, she fumbled with the cedar slab, pulled it aside, and peered into...**another empty lodge**!

BECKONING MOUNTAINS

...When The Son left the beach after searching in vain for his Princess, he made a slow, sad trip back to the valley. The shock of his discovery at the village, and his concern for the old Wolf left him very depressed. When he came out of the timber at last and saw no smoke at the lodge, he hurried there, afraid of what he might find. Surprised, he found the old fellow had recovered, and had let the fire burn low as the day was warm. They embraced joyfully, but The Wolf read trouble in the young man's face.

"There are no people left in our village —"

"No one?"

"Only empty lodges, cold fires, and the cry of the gulls."

"The Chief— the Princess— everyone is gone?" The Wolf had sat down suddenly, aware of the shock to both of them. Regret filled him, that he had not been able to persuade the people to come away with him at the first warning of the raiders' appearance. The faces of those he loved appeared to him, and a great sadness overcame him.

He walked outside and turned his face to the mountains — they were calling to him again. The Son was beside him now, listening as The Wolf told again about the beautiful meadow in the cleft of the far peaks with avalanche lilies and red-tail flowers. He proposed that they set out now on a hunting trip, his favorite cure for any problem.

"When you see the beautiful little lake, you will be glad. You will forget your troubles." The Son could not answer, he needed time to think. After a few days' hunting nearby, The Wolf declared he was ready to go to the mountains again. The Son, still very depressed, felt no desire to go with The Wolf. The old man left one morning, promising to return in a few days.

To keep up his spirits, The Son worked on the lodge, gathering armloads of moss, and chinking the walls to insulate the lodge against the coming winter cold. The Wolf had pointed out a big cedar tree that had fallen and shattered. There was one large section suitable for a slab to make a door. By burning and splitting the slab with wedges, he made it into a door that could easily be pushed to one side.

He watched now for The Wolf to return. It had been more than 'a few days' and he still had not appeared. The Son began to worry about him, fearing that he may have become ill again. The huckleberries were beginning to turn blue, which meant that it was time for the salmon, and colder days would soon come. One morning, he awoke to find a familiar sharpness in the air, and he made his decision to start out to find The Wolf. Because the old man had learned the value of leaving a carefully marked trail, The Son easily followed him to the little meadow high in the mountains. He found the tiny lake — quiet and jewel-like — just as The Wolf had said. He felt like an intruder into the peacefulness of the setting. It was so lovely that he immediately thought of his Princess — how she would have loved it.

He found a brush shelter which The Wolf had built, but he also realized it had not been used for some time. The Son made camp there and waited for several days, and still The Wolf did not come. There were deer and elk all around, and it was here that The Son killed his first elk, a fine yearling. He was elated, and wanted The

Wolf to see what he had done. The two of them could carry out an ample supply of dried meat for the winter.

Quickly the nights became colder, and with these signs of autumn, the deer and elk began to leave for the low country. The first snow could come at any time. 'The Wolf knows that the season of coldness is coming — why has he not come back?' The Son decided to wait one more day, and if The Wolf had not returned by then, he would make up a load of the elk meat and start down the mountain...

...The Princess had made the tiring and fearful trip from the beach to be with her loved one again. Her disappointment in missing him at the lodge was not only bitter, but it aroused the fears and heartache of being alone again — this time in a strange place. After a time of weeping, she stood up and went outside to look at her surroundings—so beautiful! The stream, the meadows, and the mountains were so much nearer now. Back inside the lodge she looked at the things The Wolf and The Son had brought with them from the beach. Overhead hung a bundle of deerskins and many smoked trout. In her first disappointment of finding a deserted lodge, she had not really seen nor cared about evidence of comfort and provisions about the place. Her spirits lifted as familiar touches of the hunters' handiwork caught her eye, and she built up a good fire. It began to feel and look like a home. She felt she would be safe and warm here until they returned. They must have gone hunting as they had done so many times before, and would be returning at any time. Maybe they would see the smoke from her fire and come home **today**! (She played this game with herself over and over, it made her feel better.) She made a broom of cedar boughs, and started sweeping the lodge and putting things in order.

Outside she found a big pile of firewood near the entrance. Looking across the meadow, she hoped to see the two men coming down the trail. She would look many times before that day was over, and still they would not come. On her first trip to the stream for water, she was delighted to find the luscious huckleberries heavy on the bushes. Now she had more work to keep her occupied.

She recalled the happy times at the village when they had picked

57

the berries and dried them for winter keeping. While women and children picked berries, the men built fires on the flat bedrock along the stream. After the fires had burned low, the rocks were swept clean and the berries spread on them to dry. There was no way to do that here, but the Princess would pick the berries and think of some way to dry them later. She carried the heaping baskets back to the lodge, and busied herself with her evening meal. She realized she was beginning to feel at home in the new place.

As the evening shadows grew longer, she took one last look across the meadow, hoping to see the hunters, but there was no one. Closing the lodge entrance, she made herself comfortable for the coming night. She had not had much sleep the night before on the island, but tonight she would feel much safer inside the warm lodge. To fight the loneliness, she kept listening for sounds of the returning men. She lay awake by the fire into the late hours before the pleasing song of the stream lulled her to sleep.

She had a moment of fright upon waking in the morning before recognizing her new surroundings. There were a few live coals in the fire which she quickly fanned back to life. After her morning meal, she took one of the baskets to the berry patch by the stream and began to pick again. When it was full she spread some of the cedar mats on the grass and poured the berries onto them to dry in the sun. Then she contrived a crude shelf inside the lodge next to the fire, where more berries could be dried. During the next few days this task kept her hands occupied, but she kept thinking of The Son and The Wolf and how pleased they would be with what she had done. As another night passed, her concern grew.

Recalling how all the other people had gone out of her life, she began to fear that The Son and The Wolf were gone, too. One day, while looking at the distant mountains, there came an urge to go looking for the hunters. Each day the idea grew stronger, and the loneliness harder to bear, until one morning she made up her pack for travel, and set out to find them.

AVALANCHE

Out in the meadow she came to the game trail, the same one she had
followed into the valley. It led toward the foothills. She followed it
until it forked, with one path leading straight ahead into a timbered
area, and the other turning to her right and leading up a slope, which
was almost barren of trees. Her old fear of the forest was enough to
help her choose the one going up the slope, and soon she was able to
look sharply downward to the meadow. She had never been on land
higher than the bluff at the beach, and was astonished at the view

59

below her. She could see where the stream came from a big pool at the base of a rocky cliff, and then wandered across the meadows close to the big tree and the lodge. Stopping to rest, she gazed at the view below and wondered what other strange sights awaited her.

An exciting moment came as she rounded a bend in the trail and came face to face with a small band of elk! They gave her a startled look and thundered over a ridge out of sight to her left.

Turning back to the trail she came to a place where the trail crossed a narrow gulley. For ages, sand, gravel, and loose shale had been washing down this gulley during storms and spring runoffs. Seeing nothing unusual about it, the Princess stepped into the gulley where the trail crossed. Instantly she fell as her foot sank into the soft mixture. Surprised and frightened she tried to get to her feet but could not move. Everything she touched joined in one moving mass, becoming part of a small avalanche — she was riding it down the steep slope! A quick glance showed the avalanche growing in size, rushing toward the rim of a deep canyon below. Struggling frantically to get to firm ground, the Princess rode the sliding rubble downward, and went flying over the rim of the canyon — down, down — rocks and gravel scraping her body, sand and dirt in her eyes and mouth.

Beginning at the stream's edge in the bottom of the canyon, a fan-shaped pile of rock and debris had been building up for centuries, forming a knife-tip edge just under the rim of the canyon. It was this edge that caught the Princess and cushioned her fall as she rolled over the rim. The weight of her body striking the pile caused the point to crumble, and a second slide was activated. Bewildered and terrified, she rode the second slide downward to a stream in the canyon floor, and came to rest lying partly in the cold water.

Miraculously uninjured, but in shock, she lay motionless until the chill of the water forced her to crawl slowly out onto the sun-warmed shale. Praying that the earth had stopped moving, she raised up and looked about. Her rolled-up mat was caught in salmonberry bushes at the water's edge. Her spear was just beyond. Looking up at the canyon rim, she could see little chance of getting back to the trail at that point. Crawling to her pack and spear, she tried to stand but was trembling so badly that she crawled instead to a grassy spot beside the stream. She was not really hurt, but bruised, scared, and unable to comprehend the strange and unexpected events which brought her there.

Steep slopes with thick brush lined both sides of the stream. The slopes led upward to vertical rocky cliffs at the rim of the canyon. From where she sat, there appeared to be no escape. Nearby was a clump of small, bushy cedars. It looked like a good camping place and chance to dry off. She was able to stand now, and began gathering dry wood from a dead tree. Using The Son's firemaking spindle from her pack, she built a fire. A light rain began to fall, but the cedars offered good shelter.

She prepared a few dried fish and herb teas for her meal, and began to feel stronger and able to walk about without trembling. She wanted to get back to the lodge, and wondered where the stream might lead. She followed it a short distance, and found that it ran into a big whirlpool at the base of a cliff. She knew the stream came out into the big pool in the meadows, but there was no way for her to get there! Slowly she made her way back to the cedar grove. Tomorrow she must find a way to get out of the canyon and back to the lodge.

Collecting a supply of wood for a night fire, the Princess made herself as comfortable as possible. Some rain dripped through the cedar branches, but she relaxed with the warmth of the fire on her face as night closed around her. During the night she slept fitfully, and was sure she heard the old familiar sounds of surf. At long last, morning came, and sounds — real or imagined — persisted. She was puzzled; so many things were happening, and she did not know what to expect next.

The rain had stopped, and the sky was much lighter. She ate quickly, determined to find a way out of the canyon. Going upstream she found her way blocked by a big spruce log. After climbing over it and walking a little farther upstream, she could hear the strange sound growing louder. It frightened her, but her plan to get away from the place caused her to push on.

Then as she came slowly around a bend in the stream, she saw — her first **waterfall**. It took her a moment to understand what she was seeing. It looked like the stream fell from the sky. Now she understood why the sound reminded her of the surf. The waterfall was exciting, but it also blocked her way out of the canyon. In an eddy at the edge of the big pool into which the waterfall plunged were many speckled trout. Before returning downstream she speared three fat ones and took them back to her camp. As she headed back, her keen eyes searched the cliffs for an opening, but there was nothing resembling an escape route of any kind. Back at her camp she began to realize that she was trapped. The waterfall, the high cliffs, and the rocky cliff at the lower end — all left her no way out.

Putting the trout on to broil, she went again and studied the place where she had tumbled into the canyon. There just might be a chance for her to get through **there**.

'Lala-the-Good-One, you must help me to think clearly,' she prayed. She understood clearly that if she tried to climb up the face of the rubble pile, it would crumble away beneath her, so she chose to climb up to the edge, but was still far below the spot where she had slid over the rim. Standing on the crest of the pile, she found she could stretch up and just barely get ahold of the rim. Excited with the idea of freedom, her little fingers dug frantically for a firm hold. Gravel crumbled into her face, but she kept trying, doggedly. Finally she thought she had a solid grip, and was able to pull herself well up and nearly over the top. She was desperate to be so near, and lay resting for her one final effort. Just as she was about to try again, the soil crumbled in her hands, and she dropped sharply back to the crest where she had started.

The impact of her fall had been sudden and hard enough to jar loose another slide, but this time, feeling her foothold sliding away beneath her, she stepped quickly aside and watched as the avalanche raced downward toward the stream. By the time it hit the water, it was moving with such force that it continued across the stream and far up the bank on the other side. When it came to rest, a swirling pool began to grow behind the dam that had just been formed.

Puzzled by this latest event and at the forces seemingly working against her, the Princess made her way slowly back to the cedars. Then she noticed that the water was backing up behind the dam, and beginning to overflow, threatening to drown her campfire! She would have to move her camp farther up the slope, but before she could do so, another unexpected act of nature occurred before her eyes. The water level had risen nearly to the top of the dam, which suddenly gave way and was swept downstream by the force of the water behind it. Trying to understand these events, she was relieved to see the stream flow had returned to normal — she would not have to move!

The trout she had gone off and left was thoroughly cooked. She ate without tasting— discouraged, confused. She lay back to rest in the sunlight, looking up at the place where she had almost succeeded — she had been so close — but it would be hopeless after the slide. Having had very little sleep the night before, she dozed off.

She awoke in late afternoon, to find that the strange set of events had not ended. First of all, the stream had become silent again, and then she saw that the whole lower canyon was now a lake. When the dam broke, most of the material in it had been swept down to the big whirlpool, and sealed it up! The canyon was filling again, and she **would** have to leave her camp. She chose a place well up the slope at the foot of the cliffs. With a new fire going, she prepared for the coming of night. She was beginning to comprehend that the canyon was filling up, but was not aware of what it really meant for her. She was still determined to find her way back to the lodge. Before the sun went down, she climbed to a viewpoint above the stream — the big spruce log was gone, and now it was too dark for her to see it floating somewhere in the pool.

The next morning she made her way toward the waterfall, where she could see the pool below, and there was the spruce floating close to shore.

"Lala-the-Good-One, once before you provided a log for my escape from the enemy; is this your way of saving me once more?" If she could get to the log, perhaps it would carry her to a place where she could climb out of the lake! She hurried back to her camp to gather her few belongings. When she returned, the log was rolling and moving with the pool's action, and invoking the name of the Good One aloud, she scrambled onto the log, clutching at a large burl. She inched her way along to where two other large burls made a swale in the surface of the log, a natural resting place for her. Later, as the log floated by some overhanging cedars, she quickly broke off some thick boughs which would offer some protection from the rain. She was afloat once more...

WOLVES

When the deer and elk began to leave the high country, The Son knew it was a signal that early winter snows could come at any time. He had been waiting 'just one more day' many times, hoping The Wolf would come back to the shelter. Now he grew fearful and concerned that the older man had met with some ill fate. He had no hope of finding him out in those mountains. He had kept busy drying the elk meat and making it into two packs for carrying down the mountain. The meat packs had created a problem — the scent had attracted wolves, and The Son heard their howls at night, each time a little closer to the camp.

One evening as he lay by the fire, still grieving for his Princess, he decided he could wait no longer and would leave at daylight for the lodge in the valley. The sky was full of shining stars as he fell asleep. When morning came, the first thing he saw was a single snowflake disappear into the ashes of last night's fire. Instantly he was wide awake — the air was very cold — and a quick glance showed a thin sheet of ice sparkling on the lake. Out of habit he looked to the spot where he had hoped to see The Wolf returning. There he saw two wolves watching him! He was not surprised— he had been expecting them, and was relieved to see only two. Placing an arrow in his bow he started toward them, and they quickly vanished in the gathering snowstorm.

Looking to the west, he could see a great white wall of snow blotting out the landscape. He had waited one day too many, and his instincts warned him he should leave the heavy pack of meat and hurry down the mountain before the snow blocked his way. After seeing the two wolves so close to his camp, he could not bear to leave the meat to them. Shouldering one of the packs and leaving the other hanging in a tree, he started on his way. Already the snow was so thick he could barely see across the little lake. As he reached the first steep slope, the dim trail was covered with white, and he had to use his heavy bow as a walking stick to make his way down the slippery incline.

He was well aware that a crippling fall could leave both him and the meat for the wolves. The snow became deeper, the pack heavier, and the footing more hazardous. Twice he fell, but was lucky both times to escape injury. By mid-morning he had some of the most difficult trail behind him, and he stopped to rest. He realized he was not making very good time if he was to get to the lodge before darkness overtook him. As he stood resting with his pack wedged between his back and a tree, he looked back and saw that the two wolves were following him. **What if there were more close behind those two?**

He moved out swiftly, finding the trail more level, with deeper snow to improve his footing, and he was setting a faster pace. At midday, he took a brief rest, and even ate some of the meat. The falling snow was so thick by now that he could see only a short distance.

Suddenly he became aware of the presence of a third and larger beast with the two wolves.

Tiny needles of fear pricked the back of his neck — he knew the increased danger in the wolves following him after dark. He struggled to get the pack up again and set off for the meadows at the foot of the mountain, moving along swiftly as possible. He looked behind him,

66

and once more counted three forms following. Now the same instincts that had warned him about them began to suggest ways to outwit them. He could cache the meat in a tree, but he thought there must be a better way to save it. His mind was working as he pushed on down the trail. The pack grew heavier but he was determined not to lighten it. Another backward glance showed the animals becoming bolder and closing the gap between them. He debated about using his bow and arrow to drive them away. This could cost him precious travel time, and they would still be a threat in the dark.

He trudged on until he came to a long, open space with a thick clump of evergreens in it. Altering his course, he planned to pass close to them. It seemed ready-made for the plan he had in mind — he was not sure it would work but was ready to try. As he came abreast the thicket, he slipped off the pack, and leaving it in plain sight, went into the thicket. Turning around he knelt down facing the pack, and put an arrow to his bow. Through a slit in the branches, he saw the wolves had stopped a short distance off. As he watched them the two smaller wolves began to circle around behind him. The big one stood still, watching. Suddenly the two appeared on his left and moved up to the meat. Now the big wolf also took a few steps toward the meat and then stopped, looking toward the thicket.

As The Son waited for some action, he became anxious — darkness was coming on. The two small wolves moved in on the meat pack, sniffing and growling low in their throats. The big one gave a warning growl as one of them circled the pack. The smell was strong and tempting, and one wolf was now close enough to nose it. With that the big wolf gave an angry snarl and charged them savagely. Instantly the two retreated, and as the big animal turned to face the thicket, one of The Son's arrows drove deep into his chest. The animal flew into a whirling, gnashing frenzy as he tried to rid himself of the burning arrow. When The Son came out of the thicket with another arrow in his bow, the big beast struggled away, leaving a crimson mark in the snow. The others were nowhere to be seen.

Lifting the pack once more, The Son set off for the meadows. He had nothing to fear from those wolves now, he told himself, and he concentrated on his footing along the trail. He hoped to reach the lodge before nightfall as other wolves might come. It was dark by the time he came to the meadows, and he was barely able to follow the trail. When he finally staggered up to the lodge, he sank down at the entrance and left the pack lying there, as he removed the door slab and went inside.

Fumbling about in the dark for the fire tools, he had a strange feeling that someone had moved them. After some time he found them and built up a fire. With the first light of the flame he found it hard to believe what he saw! He looked at the dried berries in amazement. Then he spied the neatly folded deerskin pallet with his Princess's sewing tools lying on top, and the cedar broom — everything was in order just as she would leave it. Standing in a daze he continued to look around, unbelieving until he realized beyond a doubt that she had been there! The next instant, the question: **where could she be**?

He ran outside calling her, then stood listening. There was no answer. He ran back inside and took a blazing stick from the fire to light his way around the lodge outside. There was nothing to tell him she was near, but he called again and again, listening only to the pounding of his heart. He went back into the lodge, still unsure of what he had seen. Walking about the lodge he touched the things she had touched, and tried to sort out the facts. It was plain that she had spent some time here while he had been up in the meadow, waiting for The Wolf.

In his excitement he had forgotten how tired he was. He went outside and called her many times before he had to give up and seek the warmth of the lodge. She must have spent many days drying the berries and doing other tasks about the lodge, he told himself. But where had she gone? He had never seen her anywhere but at the beach village — could she have gone back there?

Taking a water bag, he went to the stream. Another surprise: the stream was not flowing! He looked down, his mind in a whirl. He had never heard of a stream stopping, but this one had. There was barely a trickle where the little rapids had been. At the lodge once more he sat down and tried to clear his thoughts. He told himself that the mystery of the stream was not important— what he dearly wanted was to find the Princess. Sitting in a daze before his fire, with the exhaustion of his hard day's travel heavy upon him, he vowed that he would begin searching again at daybreak...'my Princess, where can you be, where can you...' he was asleep.

He awoke before daylight and built up the fire. He stepped outside and the widening light of the morning gave him courage to call her name and to search the area once more, but there was only the white stillness, revealing nothing. He could not finish his morning meal — he had no thought for food. Before he realized it he was preparing his pack to go out again.

As he closed the entrance, he noticed a few snowflakes drifting down, and he was afraid a storm was coming. He felt some reluctance to leave, but the fact that she had been there, so close to him, compelled him to start looking for her. With one last glance, he turned and hurried on his way. When he came to the place where the trail entered the timber, he carefully studied the tracks of the animals. At a muddy section of the trail, beneath some large firs, he saw prints of deer, elk, and **then** — the tiny tracks of a woman — they must belong to **her!** And they were pointed **into** the valley, not **out** of it! He found other places showing the same. Nowhere did he see a single trace of her steps leaving the valley. Now he was convinced she was near.

He was puzzled, and tried not to think of the worst that might have happened to her. He was determined to find her. On his way back to the lodge, he made a circuit of the valley, looking for more clues. Now, at the lodge the snow was coming down in thick, lacy flakes, and beginning to accumulate.

He suddenly remembered an area where he had not looked — near that big pool, and he felt sure he should go there. He stopped briefly to take some deerskin thongs from his pack and wrap them around his moccasins, tying them about his ankles. Now he was ready for the snow. With his bow ready, he set out along the silent stream. In a few pools he could see trout that had been stranded when the stream had ceased. He also saw fresh wolf tracks where they had been prowling about the pools for the fish. When he came to the big pool, there was just the tiniest trickle coming from it.

The fresh wolf tracks led to a trail going up the slope through the timber. He followed them, thinking about a deep canyon beyond the cliffs at the pool, which he had never seen, but which The Wolf had mentioned. He would go and look down into that canyon. The idea was forming in his mind that the stream stoppage and the disappearance of his Princess might somehow be connected. If he could find what had happened to the stream, would it lead him to her?

(She had fallen and hit her head...wolves had killed her...the Evil One was putting fearful thoughts into his mind. He had been tormented by the closeness of her at the lodge, had missed her at the village, and had called so many times into the night without an answer, that he was letting the Evil One depress him.)

He climbed faster up through the timber, the snow deeper and the cold more intense. The wolf tracks began to take on a sinister look — he hoped that they had nothing to do with his Princess. As he neared the crest of the slope, the timber grew sparse and the snow deep about his feet. Standing on the crest, the curtain of falling snow was so heavy that he stared for a long time before he began to understand he was looking at a **lake**. Another mystery! So this was why the stream had ceased. But had it anything to do with the Princess and her whereabouts.?

He had about decided to go back to the lodge when he noticed a small stream flowing through the snow. It was coming from the lake, and as he stood there he realized that the canyon had filled up and was beginning to overflow at that point. The question of the change in the lake was another matter, and still seemed unimportant compared to The Son's agonizing question about the Princess. He must keep searching — it was getting so cold!

He blew into his cupped hands, and rubbed them together, a vague thought of the warm lodge at the back of his mind. Suddenly he heard the yip and whine of a wolf very near. Putting an arrow to his bow, he walked slowly toward the sound, which seemed to be coming from the edge of the lake. Standing quietly in the shelter of a tree, looking for the source of the wolf noise, he caught a glimpse of movement through the storm. Moving toward it, he saw two wolves leaping about excitedly, their sharp noses pointed at something in the drift-

70

wood at the water's edge. Supposing it to be some animal they stalked, he moved slowly toward them.

So eager were they to get at their prey, they had not seen The Son approaching. He did not want to waste an arrow on them unless it was necessary. Then one of them whirled and saw him, and they both turned and were gone! Straining to see what had attracted them, he saw no animal, but noticed something unusual about a big snow-covered log in the water. As he watched, the current pulled it toward the canyon rim and it ground to a halt.

Curious as to what had attracted the wolves, he saw some green cedar boughs protruding from the snow. Stepping onto the log, he lifted the boughs aside and was astonished to see one of The Wolf's cedar mats.! Immediately he thought of The Wolf — was this why he had not returned to the valley? Half afraid he pulled back the mat and was **stunned**! There was the still form of his dear Princess huddled in the snow. Her face was so thin and drawn, her eyes tightly closed — it was difficult to believe what he saw. With a great sad cry he lifted her up and carried her ashore.

Kneeling in the snow, he softly called her name, "Whaht Kay, Whaht Kay, my Princess", over and over, his eager eyes searching for a sign of life in her. He saw none — she looked like the people that old men said were 'gone to the land of the dead'. He refused to accept that she was dead, but filled with a cold, gnawing fear he slipped off his deerskin jacket and slid her cold body into it. Clasping her to his bare chest, he set off as rapidly as he could across the slope and down through the timber. At the edge of the meadow he stopped in the shelter of a tree to look at her, hoping for some sign of life — he could see no change. Tenderly he pressed her icy cheeks to his warm lips and begged her not to die — 'don't die, don't die —'

Holding her tightly again he ran across the meadow, frantic to get her into the warm lodge. He was unaware of the snow stinging his bare skin or of two hungry wolves watching him closely. They were not happy to have their prey snatched away just as they were about to tear it to pieces. It had never seemed so far to the lodge, but at last they were there, and he carried her in and laid her down on the pallet. Kneeling over her, he kissed her lips as gently as one would the petals

71

of a lovely mountain flower. She looked to be dead, but he vowed that if there was one tiny spark of life left, he would bring her back from the land of the dead.

The little face did not look like his Princess, but it was she, and they were together now in The Wolf's lodge. He must find a way to revive her, and **quickly**. Alternately kneeling beside her and pacing about the lodge, he was frantic to know what to do for her. How he wished The Wolf were there to help him. Overhead hung some of The Wolf's dried herbs, but instinct told him she was not ill as The Wolf had been — she was starved and frozen. The fire and the warm lodge would help the cold. He must find a way to feed her.

Taking one of the big seashells, he filled it with water and set it near the hot coals to heat. Then he found one of The Wolf's fine beaver skins and folded it into a soft pillow for her head. Again he knelt and kissed her, near weeping as he begged her to come back to life. Her moccasins appeared to be frozen, and he slipped them off and rubbed her feet vigorously. She still wore his jacket over her own, and he took them both off, and wrapped her in a warm bearskin rug, alternately rubbing her feet and then her hands.

As the water began to steam, he put in a handful of dried huckleberries to make a hot fruit stew.

"These are berries that you dried with your hands — please wake up and take some," he whispered to the Princess. Cradling her head on his arm, he gently massaged her lips and cheeks, hoping to open her mouth in order to feed her. Taking a small shell he tried to spoon some of the fruit into her mouth, but her lips would not open. Discouraged, he laid her back on the pillow and began massaging her limbs again. Suddenly he saw her lips open slightly. He tried more of the hot stew, and a tiny bite slipped through her lips, and then another, and soon she had taken the contents of a small shell' He held her to him and called her name eagerly.

It had been mid-afternoon when he carried her to the lodge. Now it was evening, and the silent body looked just as it had, but still The Son was determined and hopeful. It had been a long day since he had started his journey to the beach. He was aware of his aching muscles and the hunger, but he would not take any food until she had. As she slept, he hurried to the now silent pool for water, and brought in a supply of firewood. He closed the entrance tighter against the screaming wind and snow gusts, and was grateful for the good work he and The Wolf had done on the lodge. (Would The Wolf never return? It had been too long since he might have returned safely.)

The Son moved to the Princess's side, kneeling and taking her hands in his. Now they were only cool, not frozen as before. Lowering the elk meat chunk from the ridgepole, he cut two pieces and put them to broiling by the fire. In a few minutes the lodge was filled with a delicious, tantalizing smell. When the meat had cooked, he took his sharpest cutting tool and scraped bits of it into the hot water, making a meaty gruel. Again he lifted her head and tried to spoon some of the food through her lips. After a few attempts she had taken very little, and he gave up, disappointed. The fear of losing her gripped his heart. He placed her back on the pillow, and moved the pallet closer to the backrest so that he could sit there and lean back, holding one of her hands while he rested. The worry, the heartbreak and fear of not being able to save her would not leave him.

He lay against the backrest, dozing lightly —frightened at the thought of falling asleep if she needed him. He had not slept the night before — the surprise of discovering evidences of her in the lodge had disquieted him. Now he would let her rest a while before trying to feed her again. The night dragged on, the fire burned low, and outside the sounds of the storm faded into silence. The Son was unable to keep awake — he had fallen into a deep, troubled sleep...

... When the Princess climbed onto the log in the canyon, the first few days were uneventful, until her scant food supply was gone, and she began to starve. As the water level inched upwards toward the rim of the canyon, the waterfall slowly disappeared, and was replaced by a swift rapids. The log was subject to the whims of the current from the rapids. The current pushed the log down one side of the lake and then caused it to meander back up the opposite side. The Princess did find a piece of drift to use as a paddle, but as her strength waned she had little control of the log's direction.

On the north side of the canyon near where she had fallen into it, there was a patch of salal. The thick-skinned but sweet fruit often stayed on the vine until after the snows came. The Princess tried to get the log close to the berries, and one day succeeded in grasping a vine and bringing the log to a stop. Frantically, she picked several handfuls of the berries before the current pulled her away. The next time the log floated to that same area again, the berries were under water. She looked in vain for the chance to spear a trout — there did not seem to be any in the lake.

Her determination to find a way out of the canyon never wavered, and one day she saw the place where the water would first reach the rim and overflow. She thought that if she could maneuver the log to that point, she might be able to stand up and climb out. The idea was a good one, but within a few more days, she found she was too weak to stand! Then, to make her situation more forlorn, as she floated slowly along under the canyon rim, she looked up into the eyes of two wolves who watched her every move. They seemed to sense that she was helpless, an easy prey. Weak as she was, the cruel facts told her that her last chance for a way out was now cut off, and for the first time she thought she might have to give up her struggle — there were too many odds against her.

And then it began to snow. She huddled down beneath the cedar boughs and sank into a coma — the cold and hunger were gone, the fears quieted within her — and brilliant, sunlit scenes of her beach village and The Wolf's valley flashed before her, as she drifted gently into the Land-of-the-Dead. Her mother and father waved to her from the distance...

...He was dreaming. He must be **dreaming**! He thought he could hear the Princess calling to him from far away. Slowly he came half-awake and lay listening. There were moaning sounds coming from the darkness. Now he was wide awake. The little hand that had been in his was **gone**. Quickly he fed the fire. The first flame's light showed her twisting about as if in great agony. (Actually she was suffering through a nightmare of her last days on that log.) Taking her hands in his he tried to soothe her, hoping to see her eyes open.

She was slowly coming out of the coma, and as she neared reality, her thoughts were a continuation of the last events she could remember. Finally she became quiet and her eyes opened. Now she imagined she could hear The Son's voice. Watching breathlessly, he saw her eyes open and she stared at the firelight, seeing nothing until she recognized the flickering shadows on the wall of the lodge. She became aware that her body was warm — the terrible cold was gone, and she could hear The Son beside her.

Turning her face toward the sound of his voice, she lay staring until his face came into sharp focus. The Son watched as the faintest, but sweetest smile came across her face. Gently he raised her up until her warm face was against his own, and he felt her tears beginning to flow. They were tears of love and thankfulness — she was with her loved one again. The ordeals of the raid, of the canyon — all were behind her. It was a golden moment for both of them to treasure, and they clung to each other in sheer joy.

EPILOGUE

Under The Son's tender care, the Princess recovered quickly from her brush with a frozen death. She became her old happy self again. The young couple spent their first winter together in the big lodge in the valley which The Wolf had discovered and shared with them. They feasted on the plentiful game of the forest, and the stream supplied them with trout, crawfish, mussels and salmon. It was an easy, almost idyllic life for them.

As time went on, the loss of her mother and the Chief and the terror of being captured faded from her mind. She was caught up in providing a full life for her husband. To have come so close to losing her life, and being separated from The Son made each task she did for him all the more joyous.

The Son sometimes looked at the mountains and wondered where The Wolf was sleeping — somewhere beneath the deep snow. He had answered the call of the mountains for the last time. The Son appreciated their beauty and mystery, but they had no such lure for him.

And what of the waterfall that once been at the head of the canyon? It was now at the foot of the canyon, in full view across the meadow. At first the Princess did not want to look at the beautiful white veil of water cascading down the face of cliff and into the pool below — bitter memories of her near death were too fresh in her mind, but in time she came to love the beauty and the sounds of it.

When spring came, they made a journey back to the beach, surprising the family now in the Chief's lodge, who had given them up for dead. They feasted together and shared exciting stories of their new lives, the family urging them to stay at the village with them. The Princess and The Son could not be persuaded to remain — the valley seemed to be their home now. The family came with them when they returned to the valley, so that The Son could show them the trail, should the raiders threaten them again. The Son and the man hunted together before the people returned to the beach.

And soon it was summer in the valley. The Son took the Princess on a trip to the high meadow. She was entranced with the fields of delicate while avalanche lilies and the tiny, sparkling lake. The Son built a strong shelter in a grove of alpine fir trees, and they spent a happy time there.

The journey to the high meadow became an annual event for them, to which they, and later their children, looked forward with eager anticipation.

Willard and Camilla Morss

www.ingramcontent.com/pod-product-compliance
Lightning Source LLC
Chambersburg PA
CBHW030150200626
46812CB00016B/1774